TRIVQUIZ

GENERAL KNOWLEDGE

BRIAN WILLIAMS

A GRISEWOOD & DEMPSEY LTD BOOK

This edition published in 1991 by Blitz Editions, an imprint of Bookmart Limited, Registered Number 2372865. Trading as Bookmart Limited, Desford Road, Enderby, Leicester LE5 5AD.

ISBN 1 85605 042 4

Illustrated by Talk Back International Ltd. London.

Printed in Italy

INTRODUCTION

We think that you will find TRIVQUIZ General Knowledge as much fun to use as it was to compile. The 1,080 questions should tax your memory, furrow your brow and even make you chuckle or groan. None of them falls into the dusty definition of trivia as 'the humdrum, ordinary or commonplace'. The answers should settle a few arguments and maybe kindle the interest in tiny islands, large mammals or the origins of the teddy bear.

This book is easy to use. The questions come in groups of ten, with each group concentrating in one aspect of general knowledge, such as Food, Music, Sport, or the Human Body. Questions always appear on a right-hand page and you just turn the page to find the answers. You then move on to the next page for another group of ten questions. When you reach the group numbered 27 you will be at the end of the book (page 60). Then it's back to the beginning for number 28 (and eventually, numbers 55 and 82).

There are no real limits to general knowledge, so no one should expect to get a perfect score. Be a little bit suspicious of anyone who gets too many answers right — he or she might have stayed up the night before with a copy of the book. You can take it in turns to read questions or you can form teams. Win or lose, you'll find it fun, and if you're playing in the car, the motorway miles will slip by unnoticed.

Finally, we should issue a warning: trivia is addictive. By the time you reach the 1,080th answer you'll probably be hooked, and ready for more questions. Don't worry. Help is at hand — in the form of this book's companion volume, TRIVQUIZ People & Places.

1 GENERAL KNOWLEDGE

1 What is the first day of Lent?
2 What colour is amethyst?
3 What does an altimeter measure?
4 How many letters are there in the alphabet?
5 How many pickled peppers did Peter Piper pick?
6 What was an allosaur?
7 Where is Mount Tahat?
8 What did Alcock and Brown do in 1919?
9 Where is the world's busiest airport?
10 What drama awards are named after Antoinette Perry?

28 SCIENCE

1 Does sound travel faster through air or water?
2 What kind of machine is a crowbar?
3 What did Roentgen discover in 1898?
4 Who proposed a Theory of Relativity in 1905?
5 What did Enrico Fermi help build in 1942?
6 What have Ohm's laws to do with?
7 What is morphine made from?
8 What did Hans Lippershey invent in 1608?
9 What does a soporific drug do?
10 Where in the body is the fibula?

55 ANIMALS

1 What kind of animal was an aurochs?
2 How many wings has a bee?
3 Which animal is supposed never to forget?
4 Which animal cannot change its spots?
5 What is it that catches the worm?
6 What is a peccary?
7 Do jaguars live in America, Asia or Africa?
8 What is a black mamba?
9 Which is the biggest shark?
10 Which is larger, a lion or tiger?

82 SHIPS

1 Who sailed in the *Mayflower*?
2 Who sailed in the *Beagle*?
3 What was Nelson's flagship?
4 Which ship was sunk at the battle of the River Plate?
5 Which was the fastest trans-Atlantic ocean liner?
6 Who sailed in the *Santa Maria*?
7 What was Drake's most famous ship?
8 What was the *Kon-Tiki* raft made from?
9 Who built the *Great Eastern*?
10 Why was the 1906 Dreadnought special?

A

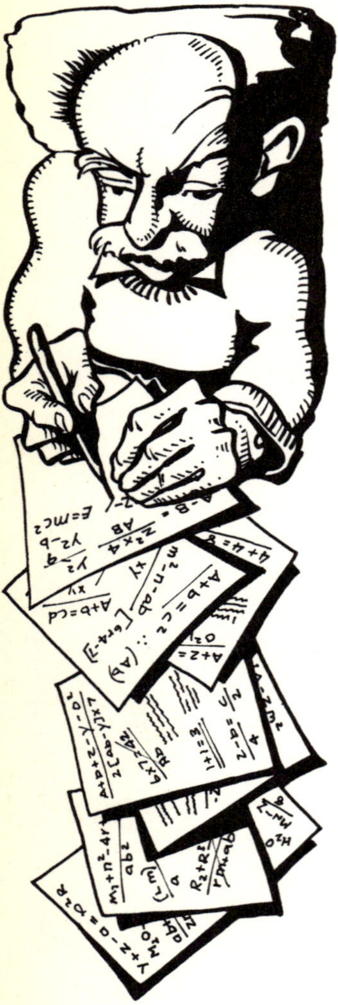

1

1 Ash Wednesday
2 Blue-violet
3 Altitude
4 26
5 A peck
6 A kind of dinosaur
7 Algeria
8 Flew the Atlantic non-stop
9 Chicago O'Hare
10 Tony awards

28

1 In water
2 A lever
3 X-rays
4 Einstein
5 The world's first nuclear reactor
6 Electricity
7 Opium
8 The telescope
9 Makes the taker sleepy
10 The lower leg

55

1 A wild ox
2 Four
3 The elephant
4 The leopard
5 The early bird
6 A South American wild pig
7 America
8 A snake
9 A whale shark
10 A tiger

82

1 Pilgrim Fathers
2 Darwin
3 *Victory*
4 *Graf Spee*
5 United States
6 Columbus
7 *Golden Hind*
8 Balsa logs
9 Isambard Kingdom Brunel
10 First modern battleship

2 *GENERAL KNOWLEDGE*

1 What is a female fox called?
2 Where was the Spanish Main?
3 Does ebony float?
4 What was an arbalist?
5 What is Meriden's claim to fame?
6 Where are a grasshopper's ears?
7 What is a bustard?
8 Who was Greta Louisa Gustafsson?
9 How did Judas Iscariot die?
10 What is the Muslim month of fasting called?

29 *SCIENCE*

1 How much skin covers the human body?
2 Which of these is a perfect number: 1,4,6,10?
3 What did Elisha Otis invent in 1853?
4 What is the chemical name for baking powder?
5 What is the chemical name for chalk?
6 Which element has the symbol Pb?
7 What is the ampere a unit of?
8 What is dentist's amalgam made from?
9 How do Centigrade and Celius temperatures differ?
10 What does concave mean?

56 *ANIMALS*

1 Where do budgerigars live in the wild?
2 What is a boomer?
3 Which is the largest of the apes?
4 What kind of animal is a cougar?
5 Which cats have no tails?
6 What is said to have killed the cat?
7 Can tigers and lions interbreed?
8 Can a dog see colours?
9 Which bear in fiction likes marmalade sandwiches?
10 What was the moa?

83 *AIR TRANSPORTATION*

1 What was the Squirt that flew in May 1941?
2 What is Mach 1?
3 What was the first man-carrying balloon filled with?
4 What engine powered the first Spitfires?
5 What kind of planes were Lancasters?
6 What first did the Comet achieve?
7 What does VSTOL stand for?
8 Which was the fastest plane ever?
9 Why is the Stealth bomber so called?
10 What is the fastest airliner?

A

2

1 Vixen
2 The Caribbean
3 No
4 A kind of crossbow
5 The centre of England
6 In its legs
7 A large turkey-like bird
8 Greta Garbo
9 Hanged himself
10 Ramadan

29

1 Almost 2 square metres
2 6 $(3 \times 2 \times 1 = 3 + 2 + 1)$
3 Passenger lift
4 Sodium bicarbonate
5 Calcium carbonate
6 Lead
7 Electrical current
8 Mercury and copper
9 They are the same
10 Curves inwards

56

1 Australia
2 A male kangaroo
3 Gorilla
4 A puma or mountain lion
5 Manx
6 Curiosity
7 Yes
8 No
9 Paddington
10 A giant flightless bird, now extinct

83

1 The first British jet plane
2 The speed of sound
3 Hot air
4 Rolls-Royce Merlin
5 Bomber
6 First jet airliner
7 Vertical/Short Take-Off/Landing
8 The US X–15 rocket plane
9 It is invisible to radar
10 Concorde

3 *GENERAL KNOWLEDGE*

1 What is measured in firkins?
2 What did Lambert Simnel claim to be?
3 What is a tarantula?
4 What nationality was Xerxes?
5 What is a Gila Monster?
6 What is an ouija board used for?
7 What were the Brothers Grimm's first names?
8 What does a numismatist study?
9 Who was Tycho Brahe?
10 Which chemical has the symbol NaCl?

30 *SCIENCE*

1 What is dry ice made of?
2 What is freezing point on the Fahrenheit scale?
3 What does a Geiger counter measure?
4 What colour does litmus turn in acid?
5 Of which gas is ozone a form?
6 What does VHF stand for?
7 How many nerve cells does the brain have?
8 What is dermatology?
9 What does a normal person have 46 of?
10 Who is known as 'the Father of Medicine'?

57 *ANIMALS*

1 Where did moas live?
2 Did wolves ever live in Britain?
3 Where is a rattlesnake's rattle?
4 What was Pegasus in Greek myth?
5 Which mythical animal could kill with a look?
6 What is a beaver's home called?
7 What do cygnets grow up to become?
8 Are glow-worms worms?
9 What is a beluga?
10 Are eels fish, reptiles or worms?

84 *TRANSPORTATION*

1 What did Detroit have first in 1919?
2 Where were the first motorways built?
3 What shape is a delta wing?
4 What comes out of a green petrol pump?
5 By what name was the B–17 better known?
6 Where a plane's ailerons?
7 Who first flew the Atlantic solo?
8 When did cars first have automatic wipers?
9 Which country gave the world parking meters?
10 Which country has the most cars?

A

3

1 Liquid
2 King of England (1486)
3 A spider
4 Persian
5 A poisonous American lizard
6 To contact the spirit world
7 Jakob and Wilhelm
8 Coins
9 A Danish astronomer
10 Sodium chloride – salt

30

1 Carbon dioxide
2 32 degrees
3 Radioactivity
4 Red
5 Oxygen
6 Very High Frequency
7 About 10,000 million
8 The treatment of skin diseases
9 Chromosomes
10 Hippocrates (about 460–377 BC)

57

1 New Zealand
2 Yes, the last one was killed in 1743
3 In its tail
4 A winged horse
5 Basilisk
6 A lodge
7 Swans
8 No, beetle larvae
9 A kind of sturgeon (a fish)
10 Fish

84

1 Traffic lights
2 Italy
3 Triangular
4 Unleaded fuel
5 Flying Fortress
6 On the wings
7 Charles Lindbergh
8 1919
9 The United States
10 The United States

4 *GENERAL KNOWLEDGE*

1 Which is the premier English dukedom?
2 What was the name of the Royal Navy's last battleship?
3 How many words in the English language?
4 Which was the first gaslit London theatre?
5 What do the initials VSO stand for?
6 Which religion holds cows sacred?
7 When were tea bags first used?
8 What were President F.D. Roosevelt's first names?
9 Is Antenne 2 a satellite, a rocket or a TV station?
10 Which cartoonist created Dogpatch?

31 *SPORT*

1 What sport did Gareth Edwards star in?
2 Name the first African soccer team to play at Wembley ?
3 What sport does Ian Woosnam play?
4 Who was George Herman Ruth?
5 What was his nickname?
6 What is the maximum 3-game score in tenpin bowling?
7 Who was Henry Cooper?
8 Which race did Mr Frisk win in record time in 1990?
9 How many balls are there on a pool table?
10 Which athletics world record has stood since 1968?

58 *WILD WEST*

1 Who was the most famous marshal of Tombstone?
2 What is a burro?
3 What was a maverick?
4 What animal family does the coyote belong to?
5 Which is the Lone Star State?
6 Where did a cowboy wear his bandana?
7 What in the West 'made all men equal'?
8 When was the California gold rush?
9 Which two railroads joined in 1869?
10 What did settlers use a straddlebug for?

85 *GENERAL KNOWLEDGE*

1 What year was southern England's Great Storm?
2 Which Brighton hotel was bombed in 1984?
3 When was the Falklands War?
4 Which Middle East leader was assassinated in 1981?
5 Who was the new Soviet leader in 1984?
6 Which Indian leader was murdered in 1984?
7 What year was the Heysel stadium disaster?
8 What was Piper Alpha?
9 From which country was Marcos expelled in 1986?
10 Which Soviet nuclear power plant blew up in 1986?

A

4

1 Norfolk
2 HMS *Vanguard*
3 At least 790,000
4 Probably the Haymarket
5 Voluntary Service Overseas
6 Hinduism
7 1920
8 Franklin Delano
9 A French TV station
10 Al Capp

31

1 Rugby union
2 Cameroun, in 1991
3 Golf
4 A US baseball star
5 Babe
6 900
7 A British heavyweight boxer
8 Grand National
9 15
10 Long jump

58

1 Wyatt Earp
2 A small donkey
3 An unbranded calf
4 Dog
5 Texas
6 Round his neck
7 A Colt
8 1849
9 Union Pacific, Central Pacific
10 To mark a claim (a tripod)

85

1 1987
2 Grand Hotel, Brighton
3 1982
4 Egypt's President Sadat
5 Chernenko
6 Mrs Gandhi
7 1985
8 An oil platform that burned (1988)
9 Philippines
10 Chernobyl

5 *GENERAL KNOWLEDGE*

1 How fast can a goldfish swim?
2 How many planets are there in astrology?
3 What closed on 31 July 1988?
4 What is another name for quicksilver?
5 How many first teeth do babies have?
6 What was Athena goddess of?
7 How many brothers did the Biblical Joseph have?
8 In Greek myth, who stole fire from the sun?
9 How many Nobel Prizes are awarded each year?
10 What would a nef be doing on a table?

32 *SPORT*

1 Which British football team plays at the Baseball Ground?
2 How many pieces are there on a draughts board?
3 How many red balls are used in snooker?
4 What nationality was the runner Paavo Nurmi?
5 What was Muhammad Ali's original name?
6 Which British football team plays at Roker Park?
7 For which country did Serge Blanco play rugby?
8 In which sport is Stefan Eberharter a champion?
9 What is the maximum 3-dart score in darts?
10 Which cricketer was known as The Master?

59 *WILD WEST*

1 Where did a cowboy wear chaps?
2 What was a sombrero?
3 What was jerky?
4 Who were circuit riders?
5 What was carried in a chuck wagon?
6 What were muleskinners?
7 What were buffalo chips?
8 Which state did Jesse James terrorize?
9 What was a mustang?
10 What was a Winchester?

86 *GENERAL KNOWLEDGE*

1 Who became the first woman leader of Pakistan?
2 Who was Hirohito?
3 In which year did Coventry win the FA Cup?
4 Who won the World Cup in 1982?
5 Who were cricket's World Cup winners of 1983?
6 Which South African archbishop won a Nobel Peace Prize?
7 When did work start on the Channel Tunnel?
8 What did boxer Lennox Lewis win in 1991?
9 Where do Selenites live?
10 Who was called the King of Hollywood?

A

5

1 About 6 kph
2 Ten
3 The last US Playboy club
4 Mercury
5 Twenty
6 Wisdom
7 Eleven
8 Prometheus
9 Six
10 Decorating it

32

1 Derby County
2 24 (12 for each player)
3 15
4 Finnish
5 Cassius Marcellus Clay
6 Sunderland
7 France
8 Skiing
9 180
10 Jack Hobbs

59

1 On the legs
2 A hat
3 Dried meat
4 Preachers
5 Food for cowboys on a the trail
6 Freight wagon drivers
7 Buffalo dung, burned for fuel
8 Missouri
9 A wild horse
10 A rifle

86

1 Benazir Bhutto
2 Late Emperor of Japan
3 Italy
4 1982
5 India
6 Desmond Tutu
7 1987
8 The British heavyweight title
9 On the moon
10 Clark Gable

6 *GENERAL KNOWLEDGE*

1 What is the first letter of the Greek alphabet?
2 And the last?
3 How many signs of the zodiac are there?
4 What was a penny black?
5 From which plant does saffron come?
6 What would you do with an abacus?
7 What do the letters R.A. after a person's name mean?
8 What is sauerkraut made from?
9 Is lignite a form of a coal or an explosive?
10 What do palaeontologists study?

33 *SPORT*

1 What sport does Wayne Gretzky play?
2 Which driver has won the most British Grands Prix?
3 What game is played at Wrigley Field, Chicago?
4 What do the letters T.C.C.B. stand for?
5 What is Madison Square Garden famous for?
6 In which British city is Maine Road stadium?
7 Which rugby nation plays home matches at Murrayfield?
8 Where is the M.C.G.?
9 Where is the Maracana stadium?
10 What starts at Putney and ends at Mortlake?

60 *WILD WEST*

1 Which Indian tribe did Geronimo lead?
2 What was a war bonnet made from?
3 What was a wickiup?
4 What did Indians do with a travois?
5 Who were the most famous Plains Indians?
6 What did Indians do with a calumet?
7 In which US state did Custer's Last Stand take place?
8 What was Custer's full name?
9 After whom was Carson City named?
10 By what name was Martha Canary more famous?

87 *THE 1990s*

1 What bit the Queen in 1991?
2 What happened on 2 August 1990?
3 Which sportsman was dubbed 'Biggles' by the press?
4 What began on 16 January 1991?
5 Who reached the Tory heights in 1990?
6 Whom did he pip in the ballot box?
7 Who starred as Michael Corleone in *The Godfather III*?
8 How did Tariq Aziz make a name for himself?
9 What post does Colin Powell hold?
10 How did Patriots take on Scuds?

A

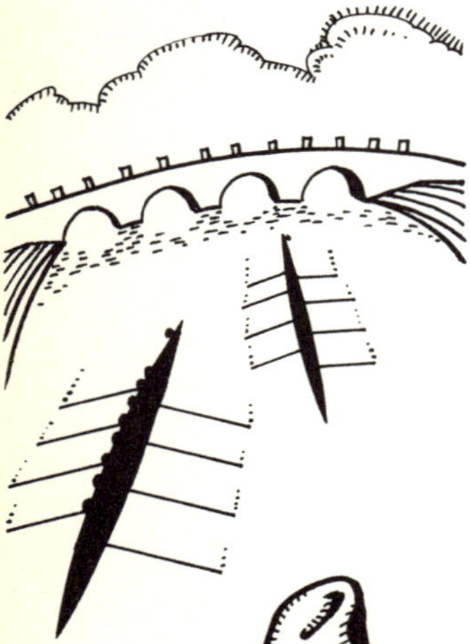

6

1 Alpha
2 Omega
3 Twelve
4 First stick-on postage stamp
5 Crocus
6 You would count on it
7 Member of the Royal Academy
8 Cabbage
9 A form of coal
10 Fossils

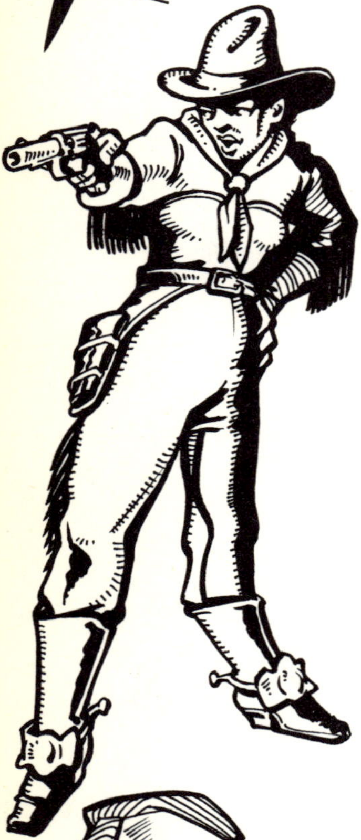

33

1 Ice hockey
2 Jim Clark
3 Baseball
4 Test and County Cricket Board
5 Boxing and indoor sports
6 Manchester
7 Scotland
8 Melbourne, Australia (cricket)
9 Rio de Janeiro, Brazil
10 The University Boat Race

60

1 Apache
2 Feathers
3 A brush house used by Apaches
4 Carry goods on it
5 Sioux
6 Smoke it: it was a pipe
7 Montana (Little Bighorn River)
8 George Armstrong Custer
9 Kit Carson
10 Calamity Jane

87

1 One of her corgis
2 Iraq invaded Kuwait
3 David Gower
4 The Allied air attacks on Iraq
5 John Major
6 Michael Heseltine, Douglas Hurd
7 Al Pacino
8 Iraq's Foreign Minister
9 Chief of the US General Staff
10 Patriot missiles downed Iraqi Scuds

7 *GENERAL KNOWLEDGE*

1 Is a Rhodesian Ridgeback a dog or a drink?
2 What measured 4 feet 8½ inches?
3 How many birds in the bush is one in the hand worth?
4 What fruit are raisins made from?
5 What is the highest rank in the British Army?
6 Who was the Roman god of the sea?
7 What was the name of Dick Turpin's horse?
8 What is a claymore?
9 How many engines does a Boeing 747 have?
10 What was a clepsydra used for?

34 *BRITISH ISLES*

1 Which city stands on the rivers Test and Itchen?
2 Where is the Royal Pavilion?
3 In which city is Tyndell's Park?
4 Which city stands on the River Taff?
5 Where is The High?
6 Where are the Backs?
7 Where are the Shambles?
8 Which city stands on the River Dee?
9 Which city has a Forest and a County?
10 Where is Shakespeare's birthplace?

61 *WHO IS IT*

1 Who was or is... Mrs Pankhurst
2 ... Mark Hughes
3 ... Chris Patten
4 ... John Glenn
5 ... James Baker
6 ... Alan Ayckbourn
7 ... Marie Helvin
8 ... Lord Mackay of Clashfern
9 ... Spike Lee
10 ... Joe Montana

88 *GENERAL KNOWLEDGE*

1 What went to war for the first time in 1916?
2 What is Mauna Loa in Hawaii?
3 Who built a bouncing bomb?
4 What is a posset?
5 When were photocopiers invented: 1930s, 1940s, 1950s?
6 What will come back near the Earth in 2062?
7 What hovered for the first time in 1959?
8 Were airships ever steam-driven?
9 What did Wallace C Carothers invent in 1935?
10 Where was the Cotton Club situated?

A

7

1 A dog
2 Standard railway gauge
3 Two
4 Grapes
5 Field Marshal
6 Poseidon
7 Black Bess
8 Scottish sword
9 Four
10 It was an ancient water clock

34

1 Southampton
2 Brighton
3 Bristol
4 Cardiff
5 Oxford
6 Cambridge
7 York
8 Chester
9 Nottingham (football clubs)
10 Stratford-upon-Avon

61

1 Campaigner for votes for women
2 Football player
3 Politician (Tory Party chairman)
4 US astronaut and politician
5 US Secretary of State
6 Playwright
7 Model
8 Lord Chancellor
9 Film-maker
10 American football star

88

1 Tanks
2 World's largest active volcano
3 Barnes Wallis
4 A drink of milk and ale
5 1940s
6 Halley's comet
7 A hovercraft
8 Yes
9 Nylon
10 Harlem

8 *GENERAL KNOWLEDGE*

1 What do deciduous trees do?
2 What do the letters UHT stand for?
3 What is a female swan called?
4 What do entomologists study?
5 Where in the body is the humerus?
6 What did Nell Gwyn sell to theatre-goers?
7 Who wrote La Traviata'?
8 Who was the first Roman Emperor?
9 What did Audubon paint?
10 Who was Sir Peter Scott's father?

35 *BRITISH ISLES*

1 Where did Molly Malone come from?
2 Where were Chaucer's pilgrims going?
3 Where was Princess Margaret born?
4 Where is Liverpool Street station?
5 In which city was the Cavern Club?
6 Which river does Belfast stand on?
7 Is Berwick-upon-Tweed in England or Scotland?
8 What industry was Macclesfield famous for?
9 Which is the largest loch in Scotland?
10 What is the county town of West Sussex?

62 *WHO IS IT*

1 Who was or is... Sinead Cusack
2 ... Leslie Halliwell
3 ... A.V. Roe
4 ... Sir Ranulph Fiennes
5 ... Devon Malcolm
6 ... Richard Dunwoody
7 ... Ayrton Senna
8 ... Chris Donald
9 ... David Hockney
10 ... Brian Epstein

89 *GENERAL KNOWLEDGE*

1 What were cat's whiskers sets?
2 Which army had cohorts and legions?
3 What kind of weapon was a halberd?
4 Who wore togas?
5 Why did Londoners flee in 1666?
6 What attacked England in 1588?
7 What crop failed in Ireland in the 1840s?
8 What is the Luftwaffe?
9 Whom did John Wilkes Booth shoot?
10 Who won the battle of Agincourt?

A

8

1 Shed their leaves in winter
2 Ultra heat treated
3 A pen
4 Insects
5 A bone in the upper arm
6 Oranges
7 Verdi
8 Augustus
9 Birds
10 Explorer Robert Falcon Scott

35

1 Dublin
2 Canterbury
3 Glamis Castle, Scotland
4 London
5 Liverpool
6 The Lagan
7 England
8 Silk
9 Loch Lomond
10 Chichester

62

1 Actress
2 Film historian
3 Aviation pioneer
4 Polar explorer
5 Cricketer
6 Jockey
7 Racing driver
8 Founder of *Viz* magazine
9 Artist
10 Beatles' manager

89

1 Early radios
2 Roman army
3 A spear with an axe head
4 Romans
5 The Great Fire of London
6 The Spanish Armada
7 Potato
8 The German Air Force
9 Abraham Lincoln
10 The English

9 *GENERAL KNOWLEDGE*

1 What did George Wells Beadle study?
2 Who flew from Germany to Scotland in 1941?
3 Who wrote *The Mousetrap*?
4 How did Sir Henry Morgan make his money?
5 What did Vesalius become expert in?
6 Who was Rudolpho d'Antonguolla?
7 How did the conqueror Tamerlane get his name?
8 Where do most historians think Columbus was born?
9 What did General Allenby capture in 1917?
10 By what name did Frederick Austerlitz become famous?

36 *BRITISH ISLES*

1 Where is Sutton Hoo?
2 What happened at Runnymede in 1215?
3 What sweeps up the River Severn on the spring tide?
4 In which county are Newlyn and Falmouth?
5 Which two old counties make up Cumbria?
6 What is held at Llangollen in July?
7 Where can visitors see the Victory and Mary Rose?
8 What is Pluckley, in Kent, famous for?
9 How many Welsh counties are called Glamorgan?
10 In which county is the battlefield of Edgehill?

63 *WHO IS IT*

1 Who was or is... Dawn French
2 ... Barbara Castle
3 ... Amelia Earhart
4 ... Evonne Goolagong
5 ... Tom Sellick
6 ... James Goldsmith
7 ... Greg LeMond
8 ... Billy Bragg
9 ... Martin Amis
10 ... Roger Bannister

90 *GENERAL KNOWLEDGE*

1 What did Mary Read do for a living?
2 What famous book did Mary Shelley write?
3 Of which country was Zog king?
4 What country's capital is Manila?
5 What is an ornithopter?
6 How many degrees are there in a triangle?
7 Where are the twin towers of the World Trade Center?
8 What is the capital of Indonesia?
9 Which soccer club plays at Highbury?
10 In which city is the University of Aston?

A

9

1 Genes
2 Rudolf Hess
3 Agatha Christie
4 He was a pirate
5 Human anatomy
6 Rudolph Valentino
7 The name means Timur the Lame
8 Genoa
9 Jerusalem
10 Fred Astaire

36

1 Suffolk
2 King John signed Magna Carta
3 The Severn Bore (a tidal wave)
4 Cornwall
5 Cumberland and Westmorland
6 The International Eisteddfod
7 Portsmouth
8 Ghosts (the most in England)
9 Three (Mid, South and West)
10 Warwickshire

63

1 Comedienne
2 Politician
3 Pioneer long distance pilot
4 Tennis star
5 Movie star
6 Financier
7 Cyclist
8 Singer
9 Novelist
10 Runner

90

1 She was a pirate
2 *Frankenstein*
3 Albania
4 Philippines
5 An aeroplane with flapping wings
6 180 degrees
7 New York
8 Jakarta
9 Arsenal
10 Birmingham

10 *GENERAL KNOWLEDGE*

1 What was the Black Death?
2 Who was the Red Baron?
3 Who are the All-Blacks?
4 Whose army is the Red Army?
5 Which British army unit are known as Redcaps?
6 Where is the Orange River?
7 What did cowboys mean by a greenhorn?
8 Who were called bluestockings?
9 What did a white feather once signify?
10 What is red biddy?

37 *THE ARTS*

1 In music what terms means very soft, softest?
2 Which is the lowest male voice?
3 How many movements are there in a typical symphony?
4 Who might wear a tutu?
5 What was Chopin's nationality?
6 When was skiffle music popular?
7 What was jitterbugging?
8 Where did calypsos originate?
9 Who wrote a poem about an Ancient Mariner?
10 On what occasion is an elegy written?

64 *SPACE*

1 How many planets orbit the Sun?
2 Which is the biggest?
3 Which has the most prominent rings?
4 Which planet is nearest the Sun?
5 Which is the hottest planet?
6 Which is the smallest and coldest?
7 Which comes closest to Earth?
8 Which was once thought to have 'canals'?
9 Which planet looks brightest from Earth?
10 How many planets have no moons?

91 *GENERAL KNOWLEDGE*

1 What is the chemical name for burning?
2 Will a candle burn in space?
3 Do sand dunes move?
4 What makes stars twinkle?
5 What is a Myr?
6 Can anything travel faster than light?
7 Where are asteroids found?
8 Who wear dhotis?
9 What kind of films did Hammer Studios specialize in?
10 What is bonsai?

A

10

1 The Plague
2 Manfred von Richthofen
3 The New Zealand rugby team
4 The Soviet Union
5 The military police
6 South Africa
7 Someone new to ranch life
8 Educated women (in the 1700s)
9 Cowardice
10 Red wine and methylated spirits

37

1 Pianissimo
2 Bass
3 Four
4 A ballerina
5 Polish
6 1950s
7 A dance popular in the 1940s
8 West Indies
9 Samuel Taylor Coleridge
10 A death

64

1 Nine
2 Jupiter
3 Saturn
4 Mercury
5 Venus
6 Pluto
7 Venus
8 Mars
9 Venus
10 Venus and Mercury

91

1 Combustion
2 No, because there is no oxygen
3 Yes, like waves
4 Our own atmosphere
5 1 million years
6 No
7 In space (they are mini-planets)
8 Indians
9 Horror movies
10 Growing miniature trees

11 GENERAL KNOWLEDGE

1 What was a Black Maria?
2 A red sky at night is .... what?
3 Which ships fly the Red Ensign?
4 What was a Brown Bess?
5 Who wrote *The Woman in White*?
6 What is a red admiral?
7 What do the Red Arrows do?
8 Who starred in the film *The Blue Angel*?
9 Which buildings have blue lamps outside?
10 What colour is a garnet?

38 THE ARTS

1 Who wrote the *Canterbury Tales*?
2 Who wrote The Importance of *Being Earnest*?
3 What does Marcel Marceau perform?
4 In what country are Kabuki plays staged?
5 Which actor's real name was Richard Jenkins?
6 Born Archibald Leach, he became a star as ...?
7 Arthur Stanley Jefferson... a fine mess. Who was he?
8 El Greco was a painter. What does his name mean?
9 Where did the French painter Gauguin go to live?
10 What was Rembrandt's nationality?

65 SPACE

1 What kind of animal was Laika?
2 Who was the first person in space?
3 How long was that first flight: 10, 108, 250 minutes?
4 What was Saturn 5?
5 How many people did Gemini spacecraft carry?
6 Which Apollo mission made the first Moon landing?
7 How many astronauts were on board?
8 Who stepped out second?
9 What first did Aleksei Leonov achieve in 1965?
10 Where did Apollo 8 fly in 1968?

92 GENERAL KNOWLEDGE

1 Who is Olive Oyl?
2 What kind of instrument is a sitar?
3 What is a group of bears called?
4 What did Mercator invent?
5 What is mah jong?
6 Where were junks made?
7 What is sake made from?
8 What does zap mean in computer-jargon?
9 What element is charcoal made of?
10 What is America's Old Faithful?

A

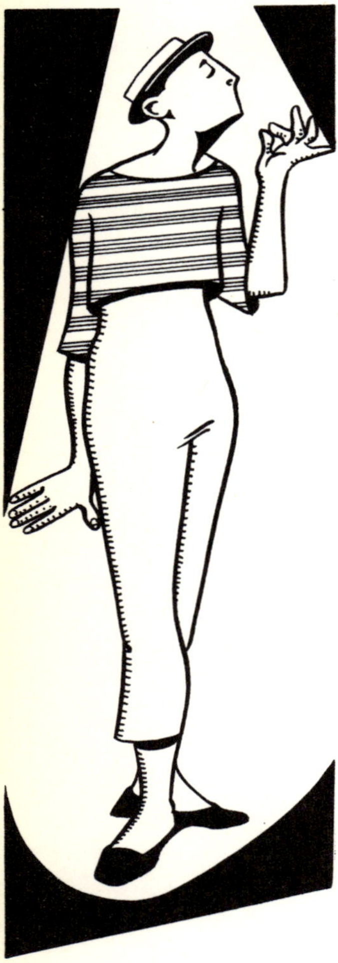

11

1 A police van for carrying prisoners
2 ...a shepherd's delight
3 British Merchant Navy
4 A musket of the 1800s–1900s
5 Wilkie Collins
6 The butterfly
7 Give aerobatic displays
8 Marlene Dietrich
9 Police stations in Britain
10 Dark red

38

1 Geoffrey Chaucer
2 Oscar Wilde
3 Mime
4 Japan
5 Richard Burton
6 Cary Grant
7 Stan Laurel
8 The Greek
9 Tahiti
10 Dutch

65

1 A dog (first animal in space)
2 Yuri Gagarin
3 108 minutes
4 The rocket on Apollo missions
5 Two
6 Apollo 11
7 Three
8 Edwin 'Buzz' Aldrin
9 The first spacewalk
10 Round the Moon

92

1 Popeye's girlfriend
2 Stringed
3 A sleuth
4 A map projection
5 A Chinese board game
6 In China (they were sailing ships)
7 Rice
8 Erase
9 Carbon
10 A geyser

12 *GENERAL KNOWLEDGE*

1 What colours make up the Swiss flag?
2 What colour is the cross of St Andrew?
3 Who were the original Blackshirts?
4 Which country awards the Purple Heart?
5 What is the Golden Rose awarded for?
6 What blossom is traditionally linked with weddings?
7 What colour shirts do Irish rugby teams wear?
8 What colour is aristocratic blood supposed to be?
9 Which is hotter: white or red heat?
10 Which are most numerous in blood: red or white cells?

39 *THE ARTS*

1 Where are frescoes painted?
2 In which country did Impressionism start?
3 What was made at Sevres and Meissen?
4 Which British architect was born in 1632?
5 What was Cervantes' most famous book?
6 How many quavers are there in a semi-breve?
7 How many Leagues Under the Sea in Jules Verne's novel?
8 What did Stradivari make?
9 How many players make up a string quartet?
10 Who wrote 'The Blue Danube' waltz?

66 *SPACE*

1 Why was Apollo 17 significant?
2 Where did Vikings land in 1976?
3 Which Soviet cosmonauts married?
4 Why was Apollo 13 unlucky?
5 Which US astronaut made most trips?
6 How long did Pioneer 10 take to leave the solar system?
7 What nationality was astronaut Rakesh Sharma?
8 What is a splashdown?
9 What is Mir?
10 Which Shuttle exploded in 1986?

93 *GENERAL KNOWLEDGE*

1 For what is the Booker prize awarded?
2 Who wrote the play *Gasping*?
3 How many years is a ruby wedding anniversary?
4 Of what sport is FIFA the governing body?
5 What car badge has a lion on it?
6 What are chub and dace?
7 What colours are magpies?
8 Who were TV's original Likely Lads?
9 What tree do acorns come from?
10 In which century were the Houses of Parliament built?

A

12

1 White cross on red
2 White on blue
3 Italian Fascists
4 United States
5 Television programmes
6 Orange
7 Green
8 Blue
9 White
10 Red

39

1 Walls or ceilings
2 France
3 Porcelain
4 Christopher Wren
5 *Don Quixote*
6 Eight
7 20,000
8 Violins
9 Four
10 Johann Strauss (the younger)

66

1 Last Moon landing (1972)
2 Mars
3 Tereshkova and Nikolayev
4 Its Moon flight was abandoned
5 John Young (six flights)
6 11 years (1972–83)
7 Indian
8 Landing a spacecraft in the sea
9 The Soviet space station
10 Challenger

93

1 Novels
2 Ben Elton
3 40 years
4 Football
5 Peugeot
6 Fish
7 Black and white
8 James Bolam, Rodney Bewes
9 Oak
10 19th century

13 *FOOD*

1 Where do gnocchi come from?
2 When are pancakes traditionally eaten in England?
3 Is Irish stew a brown or white stew?
4 What kind of food is kale?
5 What is a cross between a grapefruit and a tangerine?
6 Where was coffee first drunk?
7 What vitamins is cod-liver oil rich in?
8 What is a tortilla?
9 Where did Neapolitan ice cream originate?
10 Where does port come from?

40 *GENERAL KNOWLEDGE*

1 What, does a rolling stone gather?
2 Where do croupiers work?
3 What name is given to a dismal prophet?
4 Is a Tibetan monk a lama or a llama?
5 What date is St Valentine's Day?
6 Which king was said to turn everything to gold?
7 Which legendary bird rose from its own ashes?
8 Who was Queen of England for nine days?
9 How many rings are there in the Olympic flag?
10 What do they represent?

67 *NUMBERS*

1 How big is a lakh?
2 How many popes have been called John?
3 Which is longer: a land or nautical mile?
4 How heavy is the average human brain?
5 Women's brains are heavier: true or false?
6 How old are the oldest cave paintings?
7 What does M stand for in Roman numerals?
8 How tall are the tallest trees: 100 metres, 200 metres?
9 How fast did the first steam-jet boat travel?
10 Each month, Napoleon bathed in about 13 gallons of what?

94 *MUSIC*

1 With what kind of music do you associate Loretta Lynn?
2 What does Sir Georg Solti do?
3 What nationality was Gustav Holst?
4 Who wrote The 1812 Overture?
5 What instrument did Pablo Casals play?
6 Who sang with the Crickets?
7 Who became famous for her click song?
8 Who sang 'Ol Man River', very low?
9 What instrument does Nigel Kennedy play?
10 What is Arthur Rubinstein's instrument?

A

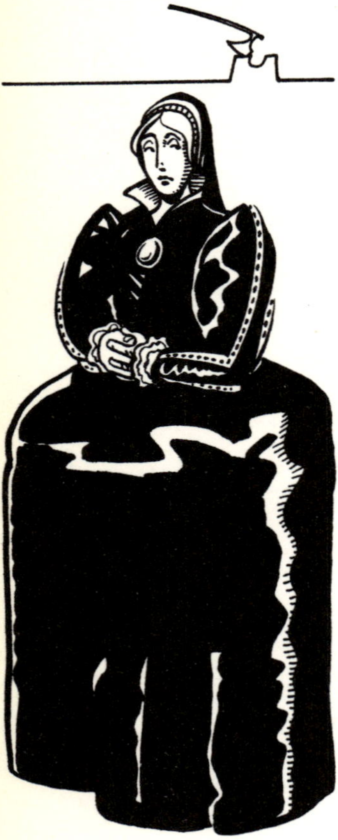

13

1 Italy
2 Shrove Tuesday
3 White
4 A green vegetable (a brassica)
5 An ugli
6 Probably Ethiopia
7 Vitamins A and D
8 A Mexican pancake
9 A cafe in Paris
10 Oporto, Portugal

40

1 No moss
2 Gaming tables in casinos
3 A Jonah
4 Lama (llamas are animals)
5 14 February
6 Midas
7 Phoenix
8 Lady Jane Grey
9 Five
10 The five continents

67

1 100,000 (used in India)
2 23
3 nautical
4 1.4 kilograms average weight
5 Lighter, about 1.3. kilograms
6 about 30,000 years
7 1,000
8 Just over 100 metres
9 6 kph (in 1787)
10 Eau de Cologne

94

1 Country and Western
2 Conducts
3 British
4 Tchaikovsky
5 Cello
6 Buddy Holly
7 Miriam Makeba
8 Paul Robeson
9 Violin
10 Piano

14 *FOOD*

1 Where does hock come from?
2 What are won ton?
3 What did 'hot dachshund sausages' become?
4 What does pizza mean in Italian?
5 Which British earl had a snack named after him?
6 What are blintzes?
7 What is tofu?
8 What meat do Jews and Muslims avoid?
9 What is smorgasbord?
10 What is filet mignon?

41 *GENERAL KNOWLEDGE*

1 How many children were born to Queen Victoria?
2 What is Monday's child ...?
3 Who was William Bonney?
4 Which animal cartoon star made his debut in 1937?
5 Who invented the jacuzzi?
6 What did Al Oerter throw?
7 When were the Olympics last held in Britain?
8 Who first appeared in *A Study in Scarlet*?
9 From which verb does the world 'coalition' come?
10 What does 'dessicated' mean?

68 *GENERAL*

1 Give the value of pi (to 3 decimal places)
2 When did the first Sputnik fly into space?
3 When did a woman first fly in space?
4 What does the abbreviation cc stand for?
5 How many centimetres are in an inch?
6 Is a yard more or less than a metre?
7 What year did Britain go decimal?
8 How many pennies were there in a pre-decimal shilling ?
9 How many pounds in a stone?
10 What was the Roman for zero?

95 *MUSIC*

1 What kind of music is Henry Mancini best known for?
2 Whose first big hit was 'Diana'?
3 What does Larry Adler play?
4 What did they call jazzmen Ory and Basie?
5 What does James Galway play?
6 Where does Kiri Te Kanewa come from?
7 Who wrote 'A Little Night Music'?
8 Whose real name is Steveland Judkins Morris?
9 Where was Bob Marley born?
10 Where was Chaka Khan born?

A

14

1 Hockheim, Germany
2 Chinese dumplings
3 Hot dogs (in early 1900s)
4 Pie
5 The Earl of Sandwich
6 Jewish pancakes
7 Soyabean curd
8 Pork
9 Scandinavian open sandwich
10 Steak

41

1 Seven
2 Fair of face
3 Billy the Kid
4 Bugs Bunny
5 Candido Jacuzzi
6 The discus (4 Olympic golds)
7 1948 in London
8 Sherlock Holmes
9 Coalesce
10 Dried

68

1 3.142
2 1957
3 1963
4 cubic centimetre
5 Roughly 2.5
6 Less (=0.9144 metre)
7 1971
8 12
9 14
10 They had no zero

95

1 Movie scores
2 Paul Anka
3 The harmonica
4 Kid, Count
5 Flute
6 New Zealand
7 Stephen Sondheim
8 Stevie Wonder
9 Jamaica
10 Chicago

15 *FOOD*

1 What are Basmati and Patna forms of?
2 What is kedgeree made from (basically)?
3 Where does Gruyere cheese come from?
4 Which Italian city gave the world Parmesan?
5 What is Feta cheese made from?
6 What colour is Leicester cheese?
7 What does 'macerate' mean in cooking?
8 What are roe?
9 What are croutons?
10 What is another name for the eggplant?

42 *GENERAL KNOWLEDGE*

1 Which Greek philosopher lived in a tub?
2 Where is the world's longest wall?
3 What travels at 300,000 km a second?
4 What did tightrope walker Blondin do in 1859?
5 Which Pacific island is famous for its stone figures?
6 In which city is the Louvre museum?
7 Where is Sugar Loaf Mountain?
8 Where is the Wailing Wall?
9 Where is the Sears Tower?
10 Why is it famous?

69 *MEASUREMENTS*

1 Which is bigger: an acre or a hectare?
2 How many seconds are there in a day?
3 How long is a millenium?
4 How fast is a knot?
5 What is measured in quires and reams?
6 How big is a hand, used to measure a horse?
7 Which is smaller: a gram or an ounce?
8 Is A3 paper larger or smaller than A4?
9 How many grams are there in a metric ton?
10 Is a kilogram more or less than a pound?

96 *MUSIC*

1 Who is Annie Mae Bullock?
2 What 1990s singing group featured Diana Ross?
3 Brian, Dennis, Carl Wilson and others became...?
4 What did Sidney Bechet play?
5 What is Bruce Springsteen's real name?
6 Where was he born?
7 By what name was Edward Kennedy Ellington better known?
8 Who wrote 'Pomp and Circumstance'?
9 What did Peter Pears do?
10 Which pop guitarist began with The Roosters in 1963?

A

15

1 Rice
2 Rice and fish
3 Switzerland
4 Parma
5 Ewe's milk
6 Red-orange
7 To soak in liquor or syrup
8 The eggs of fish
9 Cubes of bread
10 Aubergine

42

1 Diogenes
2 China
3 Light
4 Crossed Niagara Falls
5 Easter Island
6 Paris
7 Rio de Janeiro, Brazil
8 Jerusalem
9 Chicago
10 The world's tallest building

69

1 A hectare (=2.4710 acres)
2 86,400
3 1000 years
4 1 nautical mile an hour
5 Paper
6 10 cm (4 inches)
7 Gram (=0.0353 ounce)
8 Larger
9 1 million
10 More (= 2.2 pounds)

96

1 Tina Turner
2 The Supremes
3 The Beach Boys
4 The soprano saxophone
5 Bruce Springsteen
6 New Jersey, USA
7 Duke
8 Sir Edward Elgar
9 Sing
10 Eric Clapton

16 *GENERAL KNOWLEDGE*

1 What do the initials CBE stand for?
2 Who, according to the Bible, lived 969 years?
3 How many English kings have been named Edward?
4 What does 'Mac' in Scottish names mean?
5 What is the meaning of the name Sarah?
6 What is known as Old Glory?
7 Which months are named after Roman leaders?
8 Name those Romans.
9 What does the word 'hirsute' mean?
10 Who wrote 'Auld Lang Syne'?

43 *GENERAL KNOWLEDGE*

1 Who said: I came, I saw, I conquered?
2 Flying foxes are bats. True or false?
3 What did William Wilberforce fight to abolish?
4 Who was the Sun King?
5 Whose face launched a thousand ships?
6 What was David Garrick's profession?
7 What are Volapuk and Esperanto?
8 How many loaves are in a baker's dozen?
9 How did Fleet Street in London get its name?
10 Where is Harare?

70 *HUMAN BODY*

1 What acid is in your stomach?
2 How long are your intestines?
3 What use is the human appendix?
4 What causes anaemia?
5 What causes scurvy?
6 Where is your Adam's apple?
7 What part of the body does the word renal refer to?
8 Which is the body's largest gland?
9 Which gland makes insulin?
10 Do sinuses warm the air you breathe?

97 *GENERAL KNOWLEDGE*

1 Which insect transmits the disease malaria?
2 To which domestic animal is the zebra related?
3 What is a misogynist?
4 Which Dickens character dies on the guillotine?
5 And in which Dickens novel?
6 Which girl's name means 'princess'?
7 What does a cutler make?
8 Who kept goal for Northern Ireland in the 1986 World Cup?
9 Of which country was Adenauer a leader?
10 Is *The Hay Wain* a famous painting, song, or play?

A

16

1 Commander of the British Empire
2 Methuselah
3 Eight
4 Son of (Gaelic)
5 Princess
6 The American flag
7 July, August
8 Julius Caesar, Augustus
9 Hairy
10 Robert Burns

43

1 Julius Caesar
2 True
3 Slavery
4 Louis XIV
5 Helen of Troy
6 Actor
7 Invented languages
8 13
9 From the old Fleet River
10 Zimbabwe

70

1 Hydrochloric
2 About 7.5 metres
3 No use is known for it
4 Iron deficiency
5 Lack of vitamin C
6 The throat
7 The kidneys
8 The liver
9 The pancreas
10 Yes

97

1 Mosquito
2 Horse
3 A woman-hater
4 Sidney Carton
5 *A Tale of Two Cities*
6 Sarah
7 Knives (and cutlery in general)
8 Pat Jennings
9 West Germany
10 A painting (by Constable)

17 *GENERAL KNOWLEDGE*

1 What did Johann Joachim Kandler make?
2 Which day of the week is the Jewish Sabbath?
3 What is 'crossing the line' at sea?
4 Where is a scorpion's sting?
5 How many pawns are there in a chess set?
6 What part of the body does a chiropodist look after?
7 Is upstream towards a river's source or mouth?
8 What city fell to the Wooden Horse trick?
9 What sport do the Detroit Red Wings play?
10 Which universities compete in the Boat Race?

44 *GENERAL KNOWLEDGE*

1 Do giraffes have horns?
2 Which group did Phil Lynott line up with in 1970?
3 Who had a horse called Marengo?
4 What is a Blackwall hitch?
5 What was a prairie schooner?
6 What would you do on a luge?
7 When is American Independence Day?
8 How many days are there in the Islamic year?
9 For what purpose was the Taj Mahal built?
10 Who reached the North Pole in 1909?

71 *HUMAN BODY*

1 What is another name for the trachea?
2 How much blood is in the body?
3 Which is the most common blood group?
4 What happens 37 million times a year?
5 Are men's hearts heavier than women's?
6 Where is the smallest muscle: ear, hand, or stomach?
7 Do muscles make up 40% or 60% of the body's weight?
8 Do giraffes have more neck bones than humans?
9 What uses more energy, running or swimming?
10 What is inflammation of the joints called?

98 *GENERAL KNOWLEDGE*

1 What would you do with a hookah?
2 . . . and a loofah?
3 What do silkworms eat?
4 Are silkworms worms?
5 In which US state can you see London Bridge?
6 What do ospreys eat?
7 Where might you find an aquanaut travelling?
8 Does helium gas burn?
9 What was Dr Spock an expert on?
10 What is a bishop's hat called?

A

17

1 Porcelain
2 Saturday
3 Crossing the equator
4 In its tail
5 16
6 Feet
7 Towards the source
8 Troy
9 Ice hockey
10 Oxford and Cambridge

44

1 Yes
2 Thin Lizzy
3 Napoleon
4 A knot
5 A covered wagon for pioneers
6 Lie on it: it is a kind of toboggan
7 4 July
8 354
9 As a tomb
10 Peary

71

1 Windpipe
2 About a gallon (5 litres)
3 Group O
4 Your heart beats
5 Yes
6 In the ear
7 40 per cent
8 No, seven just like us
9 Swimming
10 Arthritis

98

1 Smoke it
2 Scrub your back with it
3 Mulberry leaves
4 No, they are caterpillars
5 Arizona
6 Fish
7 Under water
8 No
9 Baby and child care
10 A mitre

18 *GENERAL KNOWLEDGE*

1 What is the fastest average speed by a swimmer?
2 What kind of ship is the USS *Enterprise*?
3 What is a palindrome?
4 What kind of fiction does Isaac Asimov write?
5 What movement was founded by Mary Baker Eddy?
6 Whose son was Edward the Black Prince?
7 Who sang 'Congratulations'?
8 According to the proverb, what does absence make...?
9 How many strings has a violin?
10 What is the main food of the osprey?

45 *GENERAL KNOWLEDGE*

1 Which war lasted from 1853-56?
2 What is a grizzled skipper (apart from an old sailor)?
3 Do insects have blood?
4 Where did Great Dane dogs originally come from?
5 Where do Walloons live?
6 Which language is described as Hispanic?
7 What is the capital of Mexico?
8 Which US city became famous for quick divorces?
9 What is an obi?
10 Where do Sinhalese people come from?

72 *HUMAN BODY*

1 What part of the body is affected by otitis?
2 How many bones are there in the skull?
3 How many muscles are in the body: 212, 427, 639?
4 What is ergophobia?
5 How much of your body is water?
6 How much air do adult lungs hold?
7 Which chest muscle contracts when you breathe in?
8 Which is the longest bone in the body?
9 What is the body's main artery called?
10 Where in the body are alveoli?

99 *GENERAL KNOWLEDGE*

1 Which US marshal was shot while playing poker in Deadwood?
2 Who was the Iron Duke?
3 What sport did Lou Gehrig star in?
4 In which country is Mount Bruce?
5 Where do alpacas live?
6 Where are Skoda cars made?
7 What is a billabong?
8 In which game is a board divided into four tables?
9 In which game do players aim for three in a bed?
10 In which continent is Lake Huron?

A

18

1 5.37 mph (1990)
2 Nuclear-powered aircraft carrier
3 A symmetrical word: eg toot
4 Science fiction
5 Christian Science
6 Edward III
7 Cliff Richard
8 ...the heart grow fonder
9 Four
10 Fish

45

1 Crimean
2 A butterfly
3 Yes
4 Germany
5 Belgium
6 Spanish
7 Mexico City
8 Reno, Nevada
9 A sash worn by Japanese women
10 Sri Lanka

72

1 The ear
2 22
3 639
4 Fear of work
5 Two thirds
6 5 pints (3 litres) of air
7 The diaphragm
8 Thigh bone or femur
9 The aorta
10 The lungs

99

1 Wild Bill Hickok
2 Wellington
3 Baseball
4 Australia
5 South America
6 Czechosloavkia
7 A dried up Australian river
8 Backgammon
9 Shove ha'penny
10 North America

19 *ANIMALS AND PLANTS*

1 What is a drongo?
2 Do earwigs have wings?
3 Where do peanut worms live?
4 What is a coypu?
5 How many humps has a dromedary?
6 What is a lammergeyer?
7 What is a John Dory?
8 What do crabeater seals eat?
9 When do animals hibernate?
10 What does an estivating animal do?

46 *GENERAL KNOWLEDGE*

1 What language does the name Andrew come from?
2 Which boy's name means 'born on Christmas Day'?
3 What does 'tempus fugit' mean?
4 Who wrote about *The Railway Children*?
5 What is another name for sucrose?
6 What is a Venus Fly Trap?
7 What is another name for the cavy?
8 What can be either tip action or strike action?
9 What is trepanning?
10 Which day of the week is named after the god Woden?

73 *BRITISH ISLES*

1 Is Ireland the 11th or 20th biggest island in the world?
2 Where are the Grampian Mountains?
3 Where are the Mountains of Mourne?
4 Where are the islands of St Mary's and Tresco?
5 How many Welsh counties are there?
6 Which are England's longest mountains?
7 What is Ogof Ffynnon?
8 Would you up, down or round the Great Smoo?
9 Which is the largest lake in the Lake District?
10 Where does the Tynwald sit?

100 *GENERAL KNOWLEDGE*

1 Where would you wear a topi?
2 Which cathedral was set on fire by lightning in 1984?
3 Which poet studied medicine at Guy's Hospital?
4 In which country did Cairn Terriers originate?
5 Is a cougar a wild cat, a fish, or a bird?
6 What do Canadians call reindeer?
7 In which was was the battle of Jutland fought?
8 What is vertigo?
9 What are neon tetras?
10 Which European city is famous for its oktoberfest

A

19

1 A bird
2 Yes
3 On the seabed
4 A giant rodent
5 One
6 A vulture
7 A fish
8 Krill (not crabs)
9 Winter
10 Sleeps through summer

46

1 Greek, meaning 'manly'
2 Noel (French)
3 Time flies (Latin)
4 E. Nesbit
5 Sugar
6 A fly-eating plant
7 Guinea pig
8 Fishing rods
9 A form of brain surgery
10 Wednesday

73

1 20th
2 Scotland
3 Ireland
4 Isles of Scilly
5 8
6 Pennines
7 Britain's deepest cave
8 Down, a cave in Scotland
9 Windermere
10 Isle of Man

100

1 On your head
2 York Minster
3 John Keats
4 Scotland
5 A wild cat
6 Caribou
7 World War I
8 Fear of heights
9 Tropical fish
10 Munich

20 *ANIMALS AND PLANTS*

1 Roughly how many species of ant are there?
2 Why do desert foxes have enormous ears?
3 How many feet has a snail?
4 What is an anaconda?
5 Squids and snails are close relatives: true or false?
6 What is an eagle's nest called?
7 What are Large White, Landrace and Tamworth?
8 What is an alewife?
9 Which bird is nicknamed the sea parrot?
10 What is a female rabbit called?

47 *GENERAL KNOWLEDGE*

1 What is a coven?
2 Can penguins fly?
3 What is a loon?
4 Can birds see colours?
5 Do small birds' hearts beat fast or slow?
6 What living things have stamens?
7 Does coffee come from a nut, a bean, or a leaf?
8 What are Burmese and Siamese breeds of?
9 What colours are a skunk's markings?
10 Who invented acupuncture?

74 *BRITISH ISLES*

1 Which is bigger: the Isle of Wight or the Isle of Man?
2 Which is the biggest Channel Island?
3 In which county is Bradford?
4 Which county's name means 'village with a deer park'?
5 In which county were Lady Hamilton and Lewis Carroll born?
6 Which county will play championship cricket from 1992?
7 How many English kings were from the House of Orange?
8 Who is Baron Renfrew and Lord of the Isles?
9 How many London boroughs are there?
10 How were the Duke of Gloucester and the Earl of Ulster related?

101 *GENERAL KNOWLEDGE*

1 What artform was Barbara Hepworth noted for?
2 In which English county is Mansfield?
3 What was Little Miss Muffet eating?
4 Which car company produced the Prefect?
5 In which pantomime does Widow Twankey appear?
6 Can non-Britons win the Victoria Cross?
7 On what day does Lent begin?
8 Which Roman god had two faces?
9 What month is named after him?
10 A hinny is a cross between a horse and a donkey: true or false?

A

20

1 9,000
2 To lose heat and detect prey
3 One
4 A snake, also called the water boa
5 True: both are molluscs
6 An eyrie
7 Breeds of pig
8 A fish
9 The puffin
10 A doe

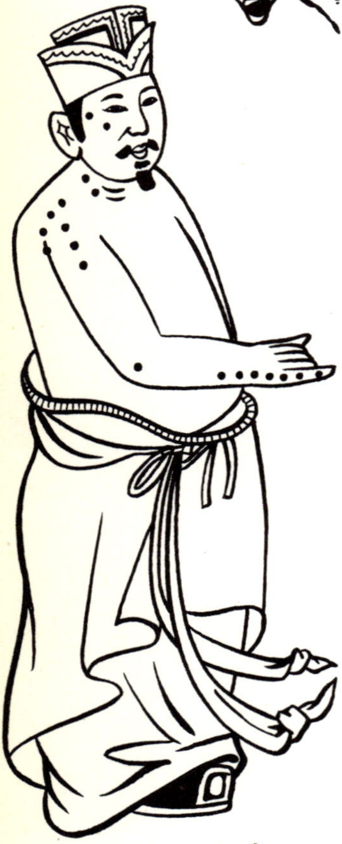

47

1 A group of witches
2 No
3 A water bird that cannot walk
4 Yes
5 Fast
6 Flowering plants
7 A bean
8 Cats
9 Black and white
10 The Chinese

74

1 Isle of Man
2 Jersey
3 West Yorkshire
4 Derbyshire
5 Cheshire
6 Durham
7 One, William of Orange
8 Prince Charles
9 32
10 Father and son

101

1 Sculpture
2 Nottinghamshire
3 Curds and whey
4 Ford
5 Aladdin
6 Yes, Commonwealth citizens
7 Ash Wednesday
8 Janus
9 January
10 True

21 *ANIMALS AND PLANTS*

1 What is arachnophobia?
2 How many legs has a crab?
3 What crops do Colorado beetles damage?
4 What is a fritillary?
5 Which is the heaviest bird of prey?
6 How many toes does a pig have?
7 What is an otter's tail called?
8 Do dingos bark?
9 Will a dingo mate with a domestic dog?
10 Which animals live in dreys?

48 *GENERAL KNOWLEDGE*

1 What is the mistral?
2 What is a cuirasse?
3 Why is bindweed so named?
4 What kind of animal is a devil's coach horse?
5 Where was Annie Lennox born?
6 Who was the ancient Egyptian sun god?
7 Which mythical creature was half man, half horse?
8 In Greek tragedy, who murdered his father and married his mother?
9 Which animals live in warrens?
10 Where is Ulan Bator?

75 *BRITISH ISLES*

1 Which prime minister married Gladys Mary Baldwin?
2 Which prime minister was born at Broadstairs?
3 Where is Queen's Island?
4 Where in Scotland is the Wallace monument?
5 Which is Scotland's oldest university?
6 In which city is Brunel University
7 In which city is Heriot-Watt University?
8 Who was born Margaret Hilda Roberts in 1925?
9 Where was the Duke of Edinburgh born?
10 Whose full names are Elizabeth Alexandra Mary?

102 *GENERAL KNOWLEDGE*

1 Who played Sergeant Ernie Bilko on TV?
2 Who played Glenn Miller in a biopic?
3 Was Frank Sinatra ever married to Ava Gardner?
4 What do the initials Q.C. stand for?
5 Where would you wear a cummerbund?
6 Which tree (in the song) has yellow ribbon tied round it?
7 In which country do Anderlecht play soccer?
8 What character did Linda Gray play in Dallas?
9 Where did Lady Godiva ride bareback?
10 Where did the Trabants car run?

A

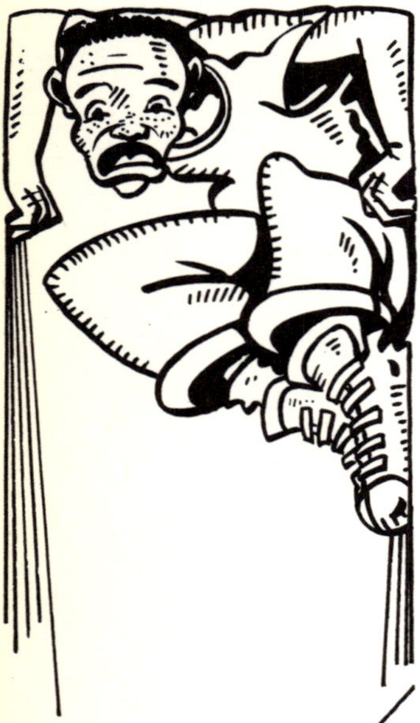

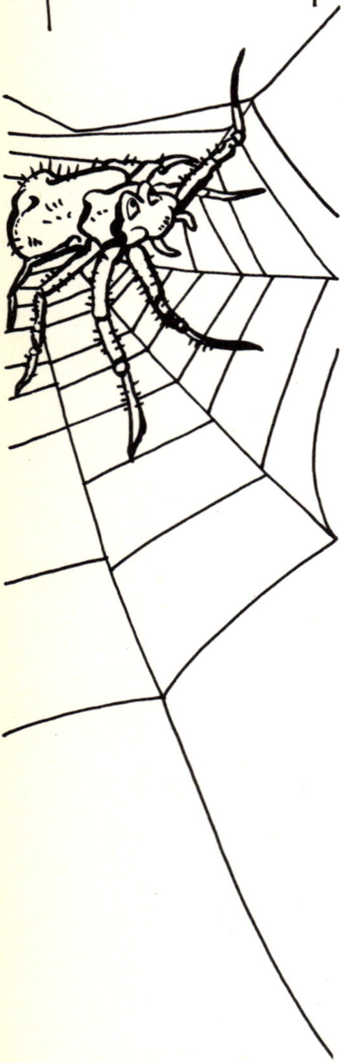

21

1 Fear of spiders
2 Ten
3 Potatoes
4 A butterfly
5 A condor
6 Four
7 A pole
8 No
9 Yes
10 Squirrels

48

1 A Mediterranean wind
2 An armoured breastplate
3 It coils round other plants
4 A beetle
5 Aberdeen, Scotland
6 Ra
7 Centaur
8 Oedipus
9 Rabbits
10 Mongolia

75

1 Harold Wilson
2 Edward Heath
3 Belfast
4 Stirling
5 St Andrews, founded 1411
6 London
7 Edinburgh
8 Margaret Thatcher
9 Corfu, Greece
10 The Queen

102

1 Phil Silvers
2 James Stewart
3 Yes
4 Queen's Counsel
5 Round the waist
6 Oak
7 Belgium
8 Sue Ellen Ewing
9 Coventry
10 East Germany

22 *ANIMALS AND PLANTS*

1 What is the tallest land animal?
2 Which land animal runs fastest?
3 Which whale dives deepest?
4 What is a Flemish giant?
5 Which is the biggest bird?
6 What are elands and dik-diks?
7 What record does the Goliath beetle hold?
8 What kind of plant is the saguaro?
9 Where did the aspidistra originate?
10 What is kelp?

49 *AMERICAN WORDS*

1 What do Americans call... lawyers?
2 ... anoraks?
3 ... bank notes?
4 ... autumn?
5 ... pigs?
6 ... braces?
7 ... underground railways?
8 ... handbags?
9 ... undertakers?
10 ... budgerigars?

76 *GENERAL KNOWLEDGE*

1 What does an oracle do?
2 What is a coracle?
3 What is a barnacle?
4 What is the Venus de Milo?
5 What is amber made of?
6 What nutrient is found in seaweed?
7 Is claret a red or white wine?
8 What is 'goodbye' short for?
9 What do philatelists do?
10 When was D-Day in World War II?

103 *GENERAL KNOWLEDGE*

1 What is a puffball?
2 What would you do with a chaise-longue?
3 Who wrote music for royal fireworks?
4 What were Manchester terriers trained to catch?
5 What did Elizabeth David write about?
6 What is measured in millibars?
7 What dog is named after a mountain pass?
8 What is ikebana?
9 What is taekwondo?
10 What is raffia made from?

A

22

1 The giraffe
2 The cheetah
3 The sperm whale
4 A breed of rabbit
5 The ostrich
6 Antelope
7 Heaviest insect
8 A cactus
9 Japan and China
10 A kind of seaweed

49

1 Attorneys
2 Parkas or ski jackets
3 Bills
4 Fall
5 Hogs
6 Suspenders
7 Subways
8 Pocketbooks or purses
9 Morticians
10 Parakeets

76

1 He or she foretells the future
2 A small round boat
3 A marine shellfish
4 A statue
5 Tree resin
6 Iodine
7 Red
8 God be with you
9 They collect stamps
10 6 June 1944

103

1 Fungus
2 Sit on it; it is a sofa
3 Handel
4 Rats
5 Cooking
6 Air pressure
7 St Bernard
8 Japanese flower arranging
9 A Korean martial art
10 Palm trees

23 *ANIMALS AND PLANTS*

1 What kind of animals were plesiosaurs?
2 Which animal has the biggest eyes?
3 Which is the longest snake?
4 What is a mouflon?
5 What is a group of lions called?
6 What are strawberry hedgehogs and prickly pears?
7 How is an ocelot's coat patterned?
8 What are Charolais and Galloway?
9 Is bamboo a tree or a grass?
10 Do wild gerbils live in deserts or forests?

50 *AMERICAN WORDS*

1 What do Americans call... drainpipes?
2 ... car boots?
3 ... caretakers?
4 ... sweet biscuits?
5 ... fairground roundabouts?
6 ... petrol?
7 ... dustcarts?
8 ... estate agents?
9 ... jumble sales?
10 ... packs (of cards)?

77 *GENERAL KNOWLEDGE*

1 What machines calculate with binary numbers?
2 What is a Portuguese man o' war?
3 How long does an adult mayfly live?
4 Would you wear a water moccasin?
5 What is the most common letter in written English?
6 Are all metals magnetic?
7 When does a colt cease to be a colt?
8 What is a gander?
9 What do the letters ESP stand for?
10 What is Earthshine?

104 *GENERAL KNOWLEDGE*

1 What sport did Greg Louganis star in?
2 What is the llama's Arabian relative?
3 What is the name of Jim Davis's cartoon cat?
4 Which gas smells of rotten eggs?
5 What game die Roy Emerson play?
6 Which old coin was known as a florin?
7 Is brioche bread, fruit or meat?
8 In which country is the port of Mombasa?
9 Which English soccer team plays at Elland Road?
10 What kind of animal is a water ouzel?

A

23

1 A water-living giant reptile
2 Giant squid
3 Reticulated python
4 A wild sheep of Europe
5 A pride
6 Kinds of cactus
7 With spots
8 Beef cattle breeds
9 Grass
10 Deserts

50

1 Downspouts
2 Trunks
3 Janitors
4 Cookies
5 Carousels
6 Gasoline
7 Garbage trucks
8 Real estate agents
9 Rummage sales
10 Decks

77

1 Computers
2 A large jellyfish
3 A few hours only
4 No, it is a venomous snake
5 E
6 No
7 After four years (males)
8 A male goose
9 Extra-sensory perception
10 Sunlight reflected from Earth

104

1 Diving
2 Camel
3 Garfield
4 Hydrogen sulfide
5 Tennis
6 Two shilling piece
7 Bread
8 Kenya
9 Leeds United
10 Bird

24 *ANIMALS AND PLANTS*

1 What do lepidopterists study?
2 How many leaves has a lucky clover?
3 What colour do stoats turn in winter?
4 How many pairs of claws has a crab?
5 Does the larch lose its leaves in winter?
6 Is the whiting a flatfish?
7 Where do fighting fish come from?
8 Why are fungi never green?
9 To which bird family does the jay belong?
10 Is a baobab a tree, an insect, or a bird?

51 *AMERICAN WORDS*

1 What do Americans call... lavatories?
2 ... queues?
3 ... the game of patience?
4 ... pyjamas?
5 ... rashers (of bacon)?
6 ... shares?
7 ... single ticket?
8 ... spanners?
9 ... sultanas?
10 ... vests?

78 *GENERAL KNOWLEDGE*

1 What is white spirit made from?
2 What are woofers and tweeters?
3 Where is Flin Flon?
4 Who discovered Hudson Bay?
5 Which people worshipped a god called Marduk?
6 Where is Ravenna?
7 Who was Eddie Rickenbacker?
8 Who is Will Carling?
9 For which country does Craig McDermott play cricket?
10 Which country's national bird is the bald eagle?

105 *GENERAL KNOWLEDGE*

1 What kind of animal is a water boatman?
2 Which revolution started in 1789?
3 In which English county is Arundel?
4 Where did Napoleon die?
5 Which was the largest all-British airliner?
6 What is botulism?
7 What does an emetic do to you?
8 Where did a wooden horse help capture a city?
9 To which family of animals do rats belong?
10 Which was the largest ocean liner ever built?

A

24

1 Butterflies and moths
2 Four
3 White
4 Five pairs
5 Yes
6 No
7 Thailand
8 They have no chlorophyll
9 Crow
10 A tree

51

1 Washrooms
2 Lines
3 Solitaire
4 Pajamas
5 Slices
6 Stocks
7 One way ticket
8 Wrenches
9 Raisins
10 Undershirts

78

1 Petroleum
2 Loudspeakers
3 Manitoba, Canada
4 Henry Hudson
5 Ancient Babylonians
6 Italy
7 US air ace of World War I
8 England rugby union captain
9 Australia
10 United States

105

1 Insect
2 The French Revolution
3 West Sussex
4 St Helena
5 Brabazon
6 Food poisoning
7 It would make you sick
8 Troy
9 Rodent
10 *Queen Elizabeth*

25 *SCIENCE*

1 What do niacin and folic acid have in common?
2 What gas makes up 78 per cent of dry air?
3 What do the letters DC stand for in electricity?
4 How big is a drop of drizzle?
5 How many sides has a snowflake?
6 What do analgesic drugs do?
7 What is a more common name for acetylsalicylic acid?
8 What alloy is made from copper and tin?
9 What is H_20?
10 What is measured on the Richter scale?

52 *SOUNDS LIKE*

1 What sounds the same as... adds
2 ... band
3 ... beat
4 ... cause
5 ... coax
6 ... cue
7 ... dew
8 ... faint
9 ... fir
10 ... flex

79 *GENERAL KNOWLEDGE*

1 What is a liger?
2 What was a blunderbuss?
3 Who was Niels Bohr?
4 Of what country is La Paz the capital?
5 What are Bath Olivers?
6 What is a nidget?
7 What did scriveners do?
8 What does simultaneously mean?
9 Is a thick-knee a bird, a flower or a complaint?
10 If you titubate, what are you doing?

106 *GENERAL KNOWLEDGE*

1 Which country's aircraft are code-lettered G?
2 What is a greylag?
3 Who played Cagney in *Cagney and Lacey*?
4 Which country awarded the Iron Cross?
5 Who was King Arthur's wise wizard?
6 Where in Britain is Snowdonia?
7 In which athletics race do runners jump over water?
8 How long is a marathon course?
9 Which premier took Britain into the Common Market?
10 Which bird in the song sang in Berkeley Square?

A

25

1 They are vitamins
2 Nitrogen
3 Direct current
4 Between 0.2 and 0.5 mm
5 Six
6 Relieve pain
7 Aspirin
8 Bronze
9 Water
10 The strength of earthquakes

52

1 Adze
2 Banned
3 Beet
4 Caws
5 Cokes
6 Queue
7 Due
8 Feint
9 Fur
10 Flecks

79

1 A cross between a male lion and a female tiger
2 An old-fashioned gun
3 Danish physicist
4 Bolivia
5 Biscuits
6 An idiot
7 Wrote
8 At the same time
9 A bird
10 Staggering about

106

1 United Kingdom
2 A goose
3 Sharon Gless
4 Germany
5 Merlin
6 North Wales
7 Steeplechase
8 26 miles 385 yards
9 Edward Heath
10 Nightingale

26 *SCIENCE*

1 At what Celsius temperature does water boil?
2 What is the square root of 100?
3 How many metres are there in a kilometre?
4 What does an ammeter measure?
5 Where are your adenoids?
6 How much does a standard medicine spoon hold?
7 What shape are the faces of a cube?
8 How many faces has a cube?
9 How many faces are there on a tetrahedron?
10 How many degrees are there in a right angle?

53 *SOUNDS LIKE*

1 What sounds the same as... gamble
2 ... guest
3 ... him
4 ... intense
5 ... lapse
6 ... manner
7 ... need
8 ... pact
9 ... peace
10 ... pour

80 *GENERAL KNOWLEDGE*

1 What is a chow?
2 What does the motto 'Ich dien' mean?
3 What do the initials EPNS stand for?
4 What is teak?
5 What is greensward?
6 What were dacoits?
7 What is a chough?
8 Where would someone have worn a belcher?
9 What is astraphobia?
10 Where is the greeting 'aloha' used?

107 *GENERAL KNOWLEDGE*

1 In which war was Mafeking relieved?
2 Does chewing gum come from a tree or seaweed?
3 What does Bob Anderson throw?
4 Which US diplomat was a child film star?
5 For which soccer club did Trevor Brooking play?
6 What is an indolent person like?
7 Which political party did Hugh Gaitskell lead?
8 In which sport might someone play a reverse sweep?
9 What are joeys?
10 When do a wombat's teeth stop growing?

A

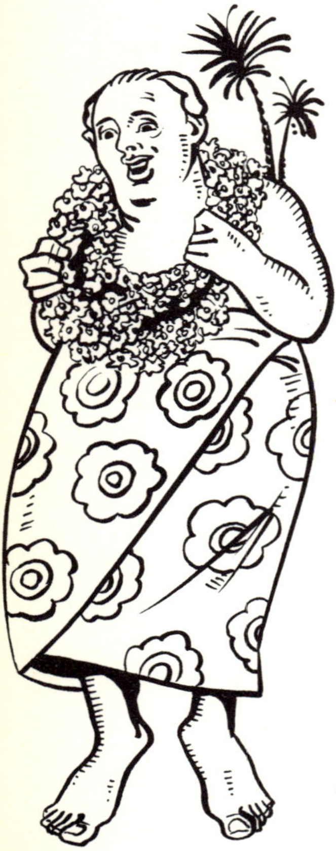

26

1 100 degrees
2 10
3 1000
4 Strength of electrical current
5 In your nasal passages
6 5 ml
7 Square
8 Six
9 Four
10 90

53

1 Gambol
2 Guessed
3 Hymn
4 Intents
5 Laps
6 Manor
7 Knead
8 Packed
9 Piece
10 Pore

80

1 A breed of dog
2 I serve
3 Electroplated nickel silver
4 A tree (and a wood from it)
5 Grass, turf
6 Indian bandits
7 A bird (of the crow family)
8 Round the neck
9 Fear of thunder and lightning
10 Hawaii

107

1 The Boer War
2 A tree
3 Darts
4 Shirley Temple
5 West Ham United
6 Lazy
7 Labour
8 Cricket
9 Baby kangaroos
10 Only when the animal is dead

27 *SCIENCE*

1 What is made from silica, soda ash and limestone?
2 What are layers of coal called?
3 What substances conduct heat swiftest?
4 What fuel is used in most space rockets?
5 Which is the lightest of all substances?
6 What is another name for reflected sound waves?
7 What revolved at 78 rpm?
8 What did Alfred Nobel invent in 1862?
9 Where do cosmic rays come from?
10 Are they long or short waves?

54 *SOUNDS LIKE*

1 What sounds the same as... rap
2 ... reek
3 ... shoot
4 ... stayed
5 ... step
6 ... soared
7 ... toad
8 ... war
9 ... wretch
10 ... yoke

81 *GENERAL KNOWLEDGE*

1 Where would you most likely find an alternator?
2 What does cruciform mean?
3 What is cribbage?
4 Is an onager a wild ass, a precious stone, or a fish?
5 Where in a building is the penthouse?
6 What do Americans call a John Doe?
7 What is a rookie?
8 Where would use a snorkel?
9 What kind of animal is a mynah?
10 What is a pennant?

108 *GENERAL KNOWLEDGE*

1 Which European country formerly ruled Angola?
2 What colour is azure?
3 Which is Shakespeare's longest play?
4 In which city were houses first given numbers?
5 Which is the longest book in the Bible?
6 What did James Burbage build in 1576?
7 Who were Flopsy, Mopsy, Cottontail and Peter?
8 What did Clarence Fender (died 1991) make?
9 What grows at roughly 1.25 cm a month?
10 How old is a centenarian?

A

27

1 Glass
2 Seams
3 Metals
4 Liquid hydrogen
5 Hydrogen
6 Echo
7 Old records
8 Dynamite
9 Outer space
10 Very short

54

1 Wrap
2 Wreak
3 Chute
4 Staid
5 Steppe
6 Sword
7 Toed, towed
8 Wore
9 Retch
10 Yolk

81

1 In a car's electrical system
2 Cross-shaped
3 A card game
4 A wild ass
5 On the top floor
6 An unidentified person or body
7 A recruit or beginner
8 Underwater
9 A bird famous for mimicry
10 A flag

108

1 Portugal
2 Azure
3 Hamlet
4 Paris
5 Psalms
6 London's first theatre
7 Beatrix Potter rabbits
8 Guitars
9 Hair
10 100